Cromer second-h[and] bookshop — 4/22

Meeting & Parting
New & Selected Poems
1941–2003

Also by Margaret Crosland

Colette: The Difficulty of Loving (Prix de Bourgogne) 1973
Women of Iron and Velvet 1976
Beyond the Lighthouse 1981
Piaf 1985
Simone de Beauvoir 1992
The Enigma of Giorgio de Chirico 1999
Madame de Pompadour 2000

Translation:
Cesare Pavese: *A Mania for Solitude*
Selected Poems 1969

Meeting & Parting
New & Selected Poems
1941–2003

Margaret Crosland

CENTAUR PRESS
London

First published in 2004 by Centaur Press
an imprint of Open Gate Press
51 Achilles Road, London NW6 1DZ

Copyright © by Margaret Crosland

All rights, by all media, reserved.

British Library Cataloguing-in-Publication Programme
A catalogue reference for this book is available from the British Library.

ISBN: 0 900001 55 0

Typeset by Glenda Pattenden
Printed and bound in Great Britain by
Woolnough Bookbinding, Wellingborough, Northants

To John Villiers Sankey

ACKNOWLEDGEMENTS

Some of these poems, now revised, have appeared in my book, *Strange Tempe*, 1946 (Fortune Press), in various anthologies, including *Poems of this War*, 1942 (Cambridge University Press); *Britain at War*, 1943 (Eyre & Spottiswoode); *For Those who Are Alive*, 1946 (Fortune Press); *Today's New Poets*, n.d., (Resurgam Books), *New Poems*, 1953, *A P.E.N. Anthology*, Michael Joseph, 1953; *Springtime*, 1953, *Springtime Two*, 1958, both Peter Owen Ltd; *New Poetry 3*, 1977 (Arts Council of Great Britain), *Shadows of War*, 1999 (Sutton), while others have appeared in *Ad Vincula*, Wisborough Green, *Canadian Forum, London Evening Standard, The Fortnightly, New Statesman and Nation, The Observer, Outposts, Poetry London, Poetry Quarterly, Poetry Commonwealth, The Spectator, The Window, World Review*.

I regret any omissions here, but it has been impossible to store copies of ephemeral magazines.

Many people have helped me compile this volume, notably John Sankey, former editor of *The Window*, who persuaded me to assemble it, Jon and Jennifer Wynne-Tyson, Vernon Scannell and Robert Greacen for their advice and help, Elfreda Powell for her editorial work, Bren Newman and Maria Colenso for their computer skills.

CONTENTS

Introduction by Vernon Scannell   ix

Part One: Cumbria

Convolvulus	1
Tea Party	2
Elder	3
The Skull of a Seagull	4
Deserted Farm	7
Season of Birds	8
The Cliffs	9
The Pheasant and the Partridge Die	10
Village	11

Part Two: Wartime and After

Empty Shells	13
Broken City	15
Statues in Winter	16
Air Raid Warning	17
Reverie at a Main Line Station	18
December 1942	19
Reported Missing	20
This Time –	21
Nurse in a Bombed Landscape	22
The Colossal Statues	23
The Delightful Ruins	24
Hampton Court	26
The Last Forest	27
Blind Man at a Party	28

Part Three: Meeting and Parting

Counsel	29
Rose in Winter	30
The Letter	31
Voyage	32
The Dark Map	33

The Gathering Dark	35
The Map	36
Noel	37
Nocturne	38
Song	39
Echo	40
This Hour was for Perfection	41
Post	42

Part Four: Portraits and Places

Africa	43
Aladdin	44
Automatic Writing	45
Portrait	47
Kew Gardens	48
Pimlico	49
Variations on a Seated Woman	50
Amsterdam	52
The White Dancer	53
Vision of Islands	54
T for Tele	55

Part Five: Celebrations and Memories

Fireworks for a Celebration	57
The Stranger Kings	58
Late Easter	59
A Band in the Park	60
New Year	61
The Smallest Orb	62
At Season's Turn	63
A Late Word for Christmas	64
The Mother	65
Sleeping on the Sofa	66
Leviathan	67
Souvenir de La Malmaison	68

INTRODUCTION

Shortly after the war against fascism ended I was living in Leeds and in its excellent Central Library I discovered a small volume of verse by a young author called Margaret Crosland. The poems in this book, which was entitled *Strange Tempe* and published by the Fortune Press, with their accuracy of observation and moments of deft lyricism were both pleasurable and full of promise of perhaps finer things to come. It has taken a long time but with the publication of this welcome selection, *Meeting and Parting*, we at last have evidence of her matured talent.

Over the years Margaret Crosland has established a reputation as a translator of and an authority on French literature and life: she has written perceptive critical biographies of Colette, Cocteau, Raymond Radiguet and Simone de Beauvoir, but her poetic output has been relatively slender. However, this selection of her work shows her to be worthy of a place among that small circle of English women poets of unassertive but authentic accomplishment, poets like Sylvia Townsend Warner, Ruth Pitter and Anne Ridler, and like each of these she has her own quietly distinctive voice.

The earlier poems dealing with wartime experience are movingly effective and she is able to capture the music and evoke the atmosphere and furnishings of metropolitan life with the same accuracy that she displays elsewhere in her evocations of the flora and fauna of rural settings. Among the wartime poems the incantatory *This Time* is a small masterpiece of verbal economy and memorable cadence.

There are poems here of personal love and loss but there is a refreshing absence of the first person singular pronoun and not a trace of self-indulgence or sentimentality. Depth of feeling is undoubtedly present but it is controlled by the artist's concern for shapeliness or form and purity of expression. This concern is beautifully demonstrated in the short poem *The Mother*. There are qualities shown in the poems in this book that are becoming rare in the poetry of today, but I am sure there is still a considerable readership ready to respond to a poetry that is honest, unobtrusively learned, unpretentious and concerned with the eternal verities. Margaret Crosland provides such poetry here and it should be welcomed by all discerning readers.

VERNON SCANNELL

Part One: Cumbria

CONVOLVULUS

The flowers I like remain invisible,
they grow from dreams and blossom in words:
all but convolvulus by the railway line,
unattainable and coolly white or pink,
still, round-faced, expressionless,
not waiting to approve or disapprove
but ready to listen.
For children this was our telephone,
bindweed that held us
more closely together
in a way no tangled wire could,
growing both loose and tight
over the cracked sleepers,
the dead bumpers,
flowering only where the trains
could never stop.

TEA PARTY

At the tree stump in the garden
the dolls sat down for sumptuous meals;
mostly I remember Winnie
with her battered black face,
fairly well dressed, with a pale blue sash,
but always in a mess, falling to bits and
often nearly thrown away but somehow
her suffering held her to me.
Mabel was chic and fair,
something of a snob, I fear,
fragile, in a white silk dress,
looking remote, inviting
my brother to shoot her;
with her upper lip gone to the pop-gun
she was never the same again,
and we cried together.
The garden was too cold for her,
she preferred the nursery fire.

But Winnie enjoyed her lunch outside,
the meaty red carnations
or eggs that were scrambly yellow daisies,
windblown petals I never found
in any other garden.

I remember too my father
coming up quietly, gazing down at the feast,
asking or rather hoping that at least
we only used the flowers that were dead.

Of course, I said, or only those that
were just, I thought, a bit dead.
He didn't scold, he could have done,
had he known, had he looked:
I think I took the best that I could find,
I knew he wouldn't say I told a lie.
I think I did, I'm sorry now.

At least, Winnie and Mabel never knew.

ELDER

In that lost village
where there are no orchards
and no allotments,
where even spring or autumn
bring little change of green or brown,
the nostalgic visitor sightsees over childhood.
Here, in the end of June,
when nettles block the well,
when bramble leaves are dusty,
the clipped sheep white and thin,
elder bursts in a flood of flower
from trees clutching the untidy walls.

The blossoms are warm, drifting against the window.

We are unashamed of sadness,
impervious to all the gibes and gentleness,
the wistful notes, hinting of ended lives
in a village of old people,
a haze of lost friends;
but children came suddenly,
pushing bicycles over the hill,
past the quarry, the elder bush
and its white promise of wine.

THE SKULL OF A SEAGULL

The skull
of a seagull
on the shore
is a more
strange thing
than its wing
in flight
or the sight
of its cry
out of the sky.

Often he dies.
His body lies
white and grey
beyond the spray
when towns know
sun or snow.
Lies now still
the harsh bill,
a flute of bone
on stone.

Miserly
the sea
must keep
this white sleep
within its care,
coldly where
the tide throws
him, goes
out and with slack
tide back.

Sometimes too
with new
bucket and spade
children made
his grave, with spells
of pale shells
about his head;
the solitary dead
assuage
the sea's rage,

So much lost
of ocean crossed,
the race
over rock-face
to cloud-climb
spanning time,
a spent
continent
in gale speed
and foam's greed.

He was not brave
to save
dream, who bought
storm, caught
a world
in his curled
lean feet;
brought no sweet
symbol, but
a heart shut.

His death
brings that breath
of one
lost sun,
the flight
of sharp light
that will fall
on all
our rocks'
last equinox.

The echo
of what we know
of sea's grey,
of sea's way,
leaving a seed
here among weed;
in the skull
of a seagull
those deaths lie
in which we die.

DESERTED FARM

No past or future from your sullen mouth,
to the bleak and automatic present tense
so endlessly beaten out from flesh and bone,
or mutely denied this heavy and waiting hand,
leaning on empty windows, sure for anger.

On the long broken smouldering land
no hardening to storm, no changing rain;
something of famine crouching in dyke or barn;
but leaves no want, no pity and no hate –
emptiness waits, the last inhabitant.

SEASON OF BIRDS

The kingfisher-diving
thought of spring
now streaks along the river,
while blue and green
comes the flash of a wing,
spinning water or sway
of iris and new-grown leaf.
The one-for-sorrow
magpie flight, now larks
bring gold to the gorse,
rekindle the purple heather,
and there by the pool
stands the tall grey heron,
watching slow fronds of green
for the silver life beneath:
the season changes
and the earth remains.

THE CLIFFS

To his careful, cold and geographic eye
her shoulders were curving cliffs near a holiday bay.
He plans the shipyard town but comes to know
the older inhabitants will not move away.

How many wharves and docks are carefully drawn,
how close is that village where they went to school.
He hates her boundary on his measured mind:
cranes will be built beside her favourite pool.

Even the calculation of a park
can trouble him now, for she, freckled and tall,
would gather sea-pinks on the grassy dunes
and count them, solemnly, on the jetty wall.

He pins nostalgia to the drawing-board.
She walked lazily over the ribbed sand,
with smooth cliffs he could almost touch and hold
beyond her always, and always near his hand.

THE PHEASANT AND THE PARTRIDGE DIE

The pheasant and the partridge die
the last of summer in their cry;
none of that beauty can deny
the season's bullet in their eye.

Though gorse and heather still defy
the pheasant and the partridge die;
pity would any word belie.
Birds that are dead have flown too high.

Killing's a game for all to try
nor waste no time to wonder why
the pheasant and the partridge die;
September else would go awry.

A patient arm can hope to buy
the sudden whirring as they fly.
Remains a silence in the sky.
The pheasant and the partridge die.

VILLAGE

When I go back, if I go back
to my grey stone village by the sea,
I think of what I'll find there now,
where no one remembers me.

I cannot lose the lasting things,
my snowdrops by the rusty gate,
the stile that led me through the fields
when the creaking bus was late.

A mountain ash, a lilac too,
children singing in the school,
a lane, a quarry, a ruined mill
and tall ferns by the pool.

Old copper mines secret in the wood,
a stone circle on the moor:
have the charcoal burners left for good?
I wish I could be sure.

A seaweed smell along the shore,
a sweep of gulls across the bay.
They haunt me often, questioning,
Why did you go away?

Flowers in the churchyard still
can hint of generations past.
Family names all carefully carved:
how long can memories last?

Sooner or later every poet
will write like this, they think they should.
All of them saying, '*I must go back…*'
If only, if only they could.

Part Two: Wartime and After

EMPTY SHELLS

The red hands took you, to the hot dust beyond
the cool village walks, climbing, riding in rain,
past Druid stones, cows at the moorland pond,
kicks at the beech leaves in the lonely lane.

Gorse fired from hill to hill, the golden curd
of cloud; sea-walls cracking, lean winds flashing
knives of foam to our throats; but you heard
the straining gates where fiercer waves were crashing.

Discussions in cold blood, meetings, delay;
your bag packed, handshakes, everyone away.

I watch the seagulls, white screams round the plough,
walk out to the low tide over the red
sand, crush empty shells, thinking of Spain, how
I grow old, and you perhaps are dead.

II

Something of spring in autumn, of brooding
on change; a deepened music in the skies,
sun striking new chords from the organ earth, moving
deep harmonies in the sea, and woods are wise.

Only our dreams are real – the leaves are dust
where we walked; now, in the blank-staring street
for those who wait, no answer, only rust
on the clutched rails, and the tread of wearied feet.

The cold dawn, aching; in the numb rain,
lonely travellers in the crowded train.

No strain for hoping now; I can reach
to stillness, with eyes Janus-like at last.
But in empty shells, picked up on the beach,
murmurs the storm to come, the storm past.

BROKEN CITY

Never to reach the final utterance
after the stumbling on the broken wall,
the struggle among the question-hands
and the lost unspeaking faces.

To wander between the brick and iron
or squint through the loophole to life
in the broken city. No words are found
to frame our barren argument.

Fret of wind in the brown trees
and each corner a dusty mouth;
the road blocked with aching silence,
or rain nagging at the doorway.

No repleteness of summer comes
to a city of shattered windows
and darkened streets, for even the stars
can see we have no penitence.

STATUES IN WINTER

In London now,
its white roofs blind against the sky,
statues are glum unruffled counsellors ,
knowing their swords frozen, assuming
an empire of plane, acceptance of calm
when generals die.

In Europe now
those distant kings, a mermaid
in the harbour, their snowy silence
answers the soldier's marble face:
'I lost that dream of liberty,'
he seems to say.

How still they wait,
nymphs and gods on the palace, how
motionless the lions. But nothing
as still as our stone voice, not even
the white roofs blind against the sky,
in London now.

AIR RAID WARNING

At nervous chattering from the city guns
torches are flashed behind the fingered blinds;
in quiet rooms lovers are lying awake,
old people put on coats and are afraid.

Anxious on silver stilts now searchlights climb,
picking their way among the cynical stars;
deep hearts of the houses throb, try not to hear
the uneasy shuffle of their basement feet.

In the emphatic blossoming of bombs
the visible cringe of steeples over
long silent streets; beneath the huddled cranes
somehow the bridges brace themselves to fight.

REVERIE AT A MAIN LINE STATION

We have all written of these,
the loud stations at night,
the endless parting and the last embracing,
the sweaty soldiers and the distant shouting,
the droop of eyes and mouth and the lifted hands.
We have all seen the world-farewell
in our myriad broken kisses,
but nothing saves the raw Prometheus
from the iron eagle of our loneliness
when the whistle darkens our separate lives.

Behind the great blank mist of eyes
what treacherous tortuous seas of grief,
boiling and coiling and curling inwards,
like the whirl and whorl of smoke
in the dark rush of tunnels:
while those we love, whose bodies are warm to ours,
whose thoughts and words build up the soul in our flesh,
now fade immeasurably far away,
a few stars in a cloudy sky of faces
and soon to be buried in the storm.

Yet can we push this darkness back,
lean on the wind and grasp the thunder,
taking our strength from love
and our will from the hatred of hate –
no other way is the clean world sped,
our own gigantic living stars
fired in the hollow furnace of our hearts:
then are the scrap-heaps of our younger lives,
Guernica, Arnhem, Buchenwald,
illumined with a richer sun,
while in our grey immediate night
long bursts of steam unleash a flight of gulls
and the shouts are a hundred larks singing on gorsey moors.

DECEMBER 1942

This autumn at least was ours;
with hopelessness or joy remember
that gusty-with-rain November,
and radiant in the dark December
days a short flutter of hours
like pigeons on a sunny roof;
passing the Cathedral every day
slowly we learnt its guardian austerity;
the gathered shapes of solemn things
darken yet dare not speak of pain.

In December with you, a world discovered,
peopled then with thoughtful beat
of rain on the empty street
the rush of invisible feet
suddenly under the trees,
or fingers careless on window or wall –
nobody came through our hidden monotone gate
and only you walked with me to hear
the rain speak its maudlin autumn tale
while the last leaves in Vincent Square were ours.

This autumn done, what strange nostalgia
will come with elusive spring again,
broken in blossom through the long-lain
secrecy of sudden rain…
easy with sunshine or shower-tangled,
how soon we may not know this ghost
companion of our starless walks, compassionate
in the long grief that we cannot lose,
for through the smouldering end of another year
we cannot see the comfort or the close.

REPORTED MISSING
For G.H.

Over our blue and idle trees
come refugee clouds from France
in the complacent summer wind.

The torn land sagging at the knees,
while fountains die in the broken towns
and the men rot, till the fires come.

Four years since you died with these,
without hope or thought of heroics,
gone out from time to silence.

There was time to take our reckoning,
all Europe dulled with racing guns,
and each day was a heavy knife.

Now with the new earth-stirring
a living spring breeds in the village
and banners blossom in the town.

You cannot know this quickening,
will not exist for those who march –
but your life is a chord in their song.

THIS TIME –
The Concentration Camps

This time the word is death
    not a cross not a lily but death
This time we saw the eyes the hands
    we know their touch their look their breath
This time the word is death

This time we marched alone
    not with friends not with lovers but alone
This time we heard a gun a bomb
    we felt the blood the soil the stone
This time we marched alone

This time they light the fire
    not a lamp not a candle but the fire
This time it burns our lips our nails
    we cling to rust to rope to wire
This time THE WORD IS DEATH they light the fire.

NURSE IN A BOMBED LANDSCAPE
A painting by Leonard Rosoman

It was all too close,
with guns too loud or smoke thick-flying:
in the glamour of destruction
we had no eyes for these dying.

This was their loneliness,
seen or talked of without feeling,
with barren commiseration
for wounds probed without thought of healing.

Grief and pride came to them
in the fire-scorch and the bomb-rending,
wandering their hollow towns
but silent of question for this ending.

Walking an empty moment,
their bodies torn from burning,
no solace can dare to come
for these in their slow and speechless yearning.

THE COLOSSAL STATUES

In the last moment of a thousand years
they speak for a speechless generation,
for those born to a clockwork sign
whose stars add up the steel equation.

Their enemy has seen them watch
the hooded falcon on his wrist;
After the long and cynic ride
these humped and hollow limbs persist.

She is no pythoness to give
them riddles for a short solution.
He warns only against their calm
before the clouded revolution.

He looks beyond their gloating mouths,
to fossils for a stranger rock.
The great river breaks in stone
through bursting gates no love shall lock

They speak to those who know the answer,
who need no moment of persuasion,
those who would probe their secret flesh
with a precise and cold invasion.

She was the richer sign of life,
symbol they thought to understand.
How shall they augur the statue's heart,
a sphinx-head in a dying land?

The riders follow the falcon back,
obey a harder, long compulsion.
The clockwork garden grows too low
to shelter them from rock's revulsion.

Here their retreat beyond simplicity,
here is the labyrinth no love shall own.
He is the Minotaur that none escapes,
she is Medusa, their eyes are stone.

THE DELIGHTFUL RUINS

We came then to a time of delightful ruins.
The town was conveniently quiet
and on Sunday mornings often
the smell of charred wood
tinged our faces warmly.
There were flowers too,
mauve and blowing in nostalgic winds,
a new enchantment for stone desolation.
The landscape had a firm dramatic shape,
hung with a sad and delicious air
far from the cosmic battle distant over the desert.
The ruins were truly delightful and lasted well.
Now they are habit, flattering to the scene.
In a ring of blackness, cathedrals and statues
have a sweet white classical taste.

But perfect like a circle grew the word now.
Now we may not watch, now there is no time.
We must all try to learn decorum.
To practise the strange purposeful faith
that houses will grow again,
complete with cream paint and geraniums.
There was never a convert to this religion,
not one. It was all accident.
Merely to take up time they planned the parks.
Somehow obstinate, nothing could stop them.
But no one has ever proved their theory.
The ruins are truly delightful,
ringed in blackness.

Watch only at night the slow march
of planet and star circling over the spires,
while earthly dancers move in a mirage
of glass dust floating over quarries,
or grey among nettles in the cellar.
Do not pretend the year is real,
the now is past as we speak, an elegant monolith
on the plain; the ruins possess, the gardens wait;
we sort the stones, neatly,

solemnly in the quiet convenient Sunday mornings,
now that the purple weeds are affection,
now that the desert is closer,
the ring of blackness tighter
upon that precious delight,
merely the ruins, unavoidable, still.

HAMPTON COURT.

'Hampton Court. This is our meeting place'. *The Waves.*

If Percival had come, we should enjoy
the lines of yews that solemnly converge
on fountains twisted in a glassy knot.
We pass the jumbled flower-shapes where
stone figures look with still surprise;
millions have died – Percival died:
convenient protagonists, they question
us to order. Why then come alone?

The formal red and white against the sky,
self-conscious chimneys and a magic clock;
in spring shone daffodils, in summer
billowing jostle of hollyhock and rose.
Peering through tall and delicate gates
the children point along the water; he died
in Egypt; he died in Greece; all deaths
are one death. The seasons bring no answer.

The picnic families lie hot and still,
watching each other; Percival has died.
He found grotesque delight in patterned swords,
high florid ceilings, talk of ghosts and kings,
loved the long gossip of the silent walls.
He is lost now to these centuries.
We thread the maze without his laugh to lead us.
We should have found the way if he had come.

THE LAST FOREST

Leading the night,
this huge hot tiger,
through its forest of stars
we thread the snake-hung dark,
reach the long moon-water, pass
warily among uncharted trees,
the tall undreamed-of continents.

Here first we know
the terrible hush of a comet's breath,
the planet like an orchid
and the lightning turned to a preying bird
with its long white cry.

Lonely and unforgiving
now we must come
to the last forest of all –
the black tiger
slips his leash and is gone.
We stand in a grass of light
and shade our eyes from anger.

BLIND MAN AT A PARTY

This one has red hair;
I'm aware of burning wire,
of something rank no perfume-cultivated
hand can stay. And with it goes
the white and waxy skin,
eyelids plump and pink, hands
all mole-mottled. I like her, she is warm.

This one is fair, she has the feel of silver.
She is cool and can be only slender.
I do not dare to touch her
lest my moist hands blur the sheen.
She is elegant, a vase for one rose,
but she is not for me.

Now I am glad, for here is one
whose company is really fun.
Her colour does not count.
She is a jumbling brown and green
as open as an English moorland,
she laughs loudly as a river.

But now is one who frightens me,
for taking her hand I cannot feel her.
Her voice is the colour of nothing,
she does not even smell of cleanliness.
She does not live, there is no love in her.
I shall not see her and I do
not need her emptiness.

Part Three: Meeting and Parting

COUNSEL

We should take counsel now with past lovers,
who walked the thorny penance path of parting
yet triumphed, strode proudly the hills of hurting
and want. Let us learn comfort, moving
in secret talk with Deirdre or Iseult,
consulting Abelard perhaps, or calling
Dante in aid. Then Bethune or Rudel
will sing of peace when other speech is cold.

Against the time when tuneless rote or cracking
parchment fall from our hands, the virelai
falter in the hall, may this tenzon
keep us close, leading each life in canzon
sure, until the heart's own hawthorn waking
from our grief shine hopeful aubade to our day.

ROSE IN WINTER

When in distant winter grew that rose,
there in that solstice grew our silent love,
sequestered light below the shrinking haws,
in roots that lay in darkness and in peace,
not in secret seed, but multi-flowering and one,
inherent in the blood, the eye in the rose
that draws its radiance from a buried sun.

And in this eye that never learnt to see
but blossomed out of blindness finding life,
here sleeps the summer of our wintered love
that coolly waits beneath the circling snow
for months to pass that cannot speed their pace,
so all the while our waiting love can grow
and in the silence learn a rose's grace.

THE LETTER

This morning I heard it
fall, lightly
but finally
into the tall red pillar,
and now when darkness comes
I think of its busy journey;
someone unlocked the little door
and pushed it in his sack,
my letter: and were there others?
But they could not matter.
Did he not see mine,
mine, the plain white
shape, did it not shine
like a paper star?
From sack to van,
through some machine
I barely can imagine,
from van to train
or ship or plane, somewhere
in a nameless room
some human hand will choose it
and take another sack or bag:
my letter will fall
with new finality
on to another floor.
The white star does not lose its glow,
can only show
how far away and farther still
lie memory, infinity.
For what did I write,
except to say
that presence and absence
are equal for me?

VOYAGE

Lost blinded love
go slowly over
the dangered sea
where rocks are smoother.

Sail warily now
through the low
green straits where
white whirlpools lie.

Cast anchor nowhere
this side of time,
nor strain the rope when
silent storms come.

THE DARK MAP

In London now when the sugared breath of spring
is coaxing blossom on our high cool walls,
your voice came from a dark map,
brought the green song of Africa swirling
round my fragile world of glass,
breaking the colour of crystal about me,
the spectre of ice from the lost raw winter:
your voice like a dancer draws me then
out of this timid April to your taut shoulder.

How shall I move to your new country
where life must splinter in the whirling water,
and the crash of stone echo a black drum?
Leave me that beast's tooth that wards off ill
and I shall find you through the molten spears.
On a day of hot rain meeting your lips' weight,
your eyelash kiss in a smoke of sun
while the lingering touch of love shall hang
in the air heavy with golden fire,
where any speech or song
is a coarse black jewel on the skin of silence –
do not speak, for your voice echoes that dark map
of love whose frontiers are closed;
in or out of that country there is no migration
for the boundary is death;
they walk there with dogs and guns,
the wire walls are barbed with poison.

But now no map will ever teach
where is that world of snow that breeds the rivers;
no cool colours can grow here, each day a flame,
each night a monstrous ruby in the brain
where blood consumes its own flesh silently.

The white greed of lilies shall swallow us both,
we shall be stars of skin on a sky of water.
Before that blindness comes to us
with clouds throbbing to a drum of anger,
before the black tides flow about our heads

and the winter world turns to that far frontier back,
do not answer, save in body speech,
let us lean closer than the lilies,
closer than all the flowers that kill,
let us move to a blaze of flesh, and love.

THE GATHERING DARK

Draw down darkness in their arms,
for these who clasp only the whole world
among their limbs, draw down down
in flowing dark, the deepest river
moulding the hills, the curled ocean.

Water is no more secret than their lips,
the green and magic moving light,
warm swirling shape grown smoother
golden and slow towards that infinite star –
the sea cracks open in their eyes.

Darkness they gathered in their hands,
watching the cool deep glistening sand
grow jewelled silence, clear as the glow
of a million amber years, where they
lie motionless, drawn round in sleep.

THE MAP

That summer now
hangs like a map beneath a light.
I can trace the marches
of our plotted kingdom,
its loyal boroughs
and tall metropolis
speaking defiance
from a chosen county.

Those little towns
of our brief meetings
flare like beacons
on high empty hills,
while quiet hamlets
of our conversation
meander along the valley,
almost inaudible now.

Through landscapes of that loving,
atlassed in hopeful contour,
our thoughts like steady barges
follow the long canals.
So, in the brittle winter,
projected still on memory,
the frozen, leafless country
awaits uncharted spring.

NOEL

A word hangs in the air,
a look floats over the fire,
a touch that is felt but never made,
all come to light in a mistletoe kiss.
No point in fighting it away, you say,
much easier to accept, like this.
I always thought I would not dare,
and never knew till afterwards:
there was no mistletoe there.

NOCTURNE

The owl cried all night in the tree.
Leaning even so close no sleep would come,
remembered warmth in a distant country.

The trees grew into the room,
their leaves hung thick in a prickle of sweat,
bright fungus mouthed beside their roots.

Flowers were knife-edged jewels in the soil,
enormous opals lingering on the wall
spread a cold taste along her flesh.

Crackle and flash of magic in glass,
smoke that was sudden in her mouth,
or the groping silent shape of cats.

White birds from fabled gardens,
stone lions with agate eyes
stood waiting angrily and close.

The owl cried all night in the tree,
dreaming that broken hot island
where vultures seized on carrion flesh.

Then came a toothed and silent face,
a head snake-haired and poison-lipped,
limbs like weeds in a black ocean.

Without waking she honed her strength,
swept down the spectral panoply
like cobwebs from a holly leaf.

Warmth took her to a different country;
leaning on love remembered she learnt sleep.
The owl cried all night in the tree.

SONG

Nearness to you
remembered as September light
on a city of blue towers.

Speaking with you,
words crossed in long-lost music
whose chords echo the spheres.

Absence from you
splinters like winter-wind, but sun
breaks in fire spun cold.

Silence with you
flings long rings of tenderness
across unsounded pools.

ECHO

Not only for preciousness of body
will I remember you,
my heart-loved –
when you are gone,
wrapped in your dark singing
down the years, and are lost,
wondering yet quieted
beyond the edge of time –
only rarely will this echo come,
stirring yet soothing
the long waters of our dream
like a single bird
flying and flown away,
leaving more solitude than was before.
So in some still and golden warmth
your voice will gather music,
come to me, and as quickly, go.

THIS HOUR WAS FOR PERFECTION

This hour was for perfection: its brief sublime
encompassed flesh and spirit with a still
yet breathless radiance. No parting chill
nor passion heat could penetrate the clime
of our September loving. To us, the chime
of planet and the word of cloud, until
the sky's octobered, cannot coin at will
that living gold, the full-moon wealth of time.

Winter now, frosting the dusk in all
our being, spectres the silence. Beyond this grey
country wanders the tell-tale path to Troy
or Rome. Not less than these, our cities fall
and only the midnight flares can light our way,
Christmas to Calvary of our bodies' joy.

POST

Sidling in a taxi down the Mall,
thinking, with darkness down over an autumn day,
when rain drowned and leaves danced,
I laughed, remembering
the state when *omne animal*
they say is sad;
yet we could talk of Wittgenstein
while sorting clothes across the bed
and if, while drinking the last of the wine
we even could agree on what he said,
in such a circumstance
is life perhaps so bad?

Part Four: Portraits and Places

AFRICA

In theatre or night-club now
his long hands wonder at his side,
invite the moment's friendship.
But when the daylight's back
the passionate committees of our hearts
betray their resolution.

His song fades, only the secret
in his eyes can haunt us,
Mumbo-jumbo, god of the Congo,
pop-star, dancer, soldier, you,
or you, tall saxophone boy,
how do we cross this deep river?

ALADDIN

Do not rub this lamp:
do not be smug Aladdin
with a dangerous hopeful smile –
O no my lovely market-boy,
remember the rolled-out rugs,
all your jumble of brassy bowls,
the glassy jewels you stole.

Do not call him back,
that tall silent ghost
in the circle of purple fire –
O no his time was pantomime
and his white-eyed grin
or the twirl of his hand
was a hint from a day-dream land.

Do not ask for wealth –
you always knew
the princess from the slave.
O no the cave's too dark to reach,
the moonlight flares in a mirror:
your lamp's not worth a new-for-old,
it will never turn to gold.

AUTOMATIC WRITING

Should I believe her crazy
that butterfly of a lady
dancing about her garden
and dithering beg pardon
to the cat?
They tell me that
she sits and writes
among the white
roses and the old tea shoppe china.
Does not believe it finer
than any other writing,
is not for ever biting
her nails to get into print.
For she has no hint
of what it is all about.
The words come to her out
of the air, fly into her pen
especially when
she ought to be washing of baking.
Somebody somewhere always making
her write, usually too
about God, Who
was never very real to her.
And on the paper words occur
she never ever heard before
and thoughts that are more
strange and grim
than ever came in any hymn
or psalm. They say
she is mad; but they
are afraid she
is a witch. Mystery
is in her hand. But who
shall know so soon
from where our words come?
Unsure of proof, some
of us are too proud
that the loud

voice is our own voice.
For the time being I have no choice,
listening to the butterfly lady
but to believe I am crazy.

PORTRAIT

The secular candle burns below her face,
she is the only silence in this place.

Down her five white centuries of youth
gathers a marble, unrelenting truth.

No one shall ever write her secret thought,
whom she has loved, what wisdom she has sought.

She is time's riddle in a golden dress,
new Venice in a painted idleness.

Question her beauty, death has no reply –
a cruel kinship falters in her eye.

She is the only silence in this place:
the secular candle burns below her face.

KEW GARDENS

People, scattered on the ground like bulbs,
grown here complete with coloured scarf and coat,
borne on a tide of blue-veined crocus, float
over lawns, swirling about the pools
and dark hanging cones of leafless trees,
encroach where sugar-pink fragile flowers climb,
draw back before the flood of lilac time
maroons them, scattered on the ground like bulbs.

PIMLICO

Speaking against the grind of trams
on a map of headlong dusty roofs,
in a latitude of trains
tracing indifferent suburbs
we met hesitant, never alone.

Between the tenements and hang-dog squares
we followed the pre-fab streets,
evening ghostly with a lamplit face,
or shouting markets parcelling up the week
into a dry unflowering Sunday.

Beyond the clocks, the boat-train dreams,
past vanished wharves whose long-lost ships
once courted islands with a magic name –
the gulls challenge our formal voices,
more lost, more dispossessed than theirs.

VARIATIONS ON A SEATED WOMAN
for Jan Le Witt

Out of a colder space the women came,
cut from jewels huge in the black earth,
out of the crystal turning ice in fire,
women whose movement knows no world
but silence only, dark as unknown stars,
cool and hard beyond the reach of eyes.
Their lines of limb forsake
the casual edge of bone
and all accepted flesh that burns away
the spectrum of their thought,
their known geometry to clasp
the still night longer.
They are all that is motionless,
sky without cloud or sea
perpetually calm, or earth
with changing season's light
forever taut and close.
In them the synthesis
of white invisible spheres
turning to make their fabled music
at the world's wall.
No detail of leaf or tree
but only the sharp words
of stone or glass
that melt in history,
explode the brain,
until the lost image of life
tumbles down,
falls here
into the absence of time.

Shaped in pearl
the swirl
of the opal-headed girl
lies in the luminous curl
to the lilac world
leaning low
on to a whirl
of unsuspected snow.

Flowers flung back to memory's urgent hand
distil black perfume in her darkened air,
turning invisible eyes to understand
the geometric moment of her hair.

Colours that sing
in kingfisher wing
on lines that lie
in the lily's eye
shapes that flow
in the ruby's glow
are caught clean,
the invisible seen,
the intangible torn,
infinity shorn,
the cipher read
in limbs and head.

AMSTERDAM

Water shall still be silence there
and houses with careful mirrors
reflect our absence. Here
where purple glass brings a white light
and bridges lead ever more deeply
into the past, barges
move slowly, bicycles fast,
towers are delicate, unexpected
and oriental beyond
red narrow houses and their trees.
Rustle of gold and brocade
is an echo on steep stairs
and here always the blue bowls
standing with pewter and darkness.
Unchanging the portraits, their modest faces;
green velvet light on smooth water
drifting under a pictured sky
thoughtfully into history.

THE WHITE DANCER

She was the solitary white dancer,
she who is always moving away,
slowly away on flawless feet,
circling the green and curving sound
with small flutter of *pas de bourrée*
as her arms reach out to distant hands,
to voices she can never answer.

She was the sylphide and the swan,
delighting in dream or loving or death,
the end of movement in her arabesque
invisible now, moving away
beyond a silent moonlit curtain
where tall, empty canvas mirrors
will never reflect her motionless face.

VISION OF ISLANDS
for Patricia Ledward

The cold edge of autumn
turns a slow blade
between sky and sea,
bares a vision of islands
opalled in cloud.

Into huge windy suns
we stride there, small
among the animal rocks,
across loud solitude
haunted by gulls.

From the green shallows
over glass-bright sand
the neat boats leave for
rose-rock shores, for legend
of saint and soldier.

Hollow now down
St Mary's Sound the bell
rings echo of wreck,
the pearls that were his eyes
and are grown stone.

The sentinel redjack
by the castle gate,
the shore's green drawbridge
to a keep of flowers
withhold the password.

Long lighthouse eyes
watching like Argus over
a hundred ships, blink
silence, testify
we are strangers here.

T FOR TELE

T for tele
but rather for time,
I should feel very
old perhaps : on the screen
I see their faces every day –
old friends, old lovers too,
the student who's turned professor,
the girl, a grandmother now.
Shall I forgive the hair that's white
or the costly dress, a little too tight?
Forgive them, yes:
they're alive, they talk,
they believe in their reality –
but the channel's wrong in time.
They forget, it's now so long
ago: we lived on songs and poems
then, for life had little else
to offer. How rich we were
and didn't know it;
how could they throw away
so much? Their game is in
the present, mine has more danger,
it lies in the past.
Each day I wonder,
how long will it last?

Part Five: Celebrations and Memories

FIREWORKS FOR A CELEBRATION

See them fly up, those living fires,
the jewelled exotic birds,
out of the darkness, the nowhere of night,
spreading a peacock's tail
over the quiet houses, the elegant parks,
over dark towns where Roman candles burn,
where thunder rolls along the streets,
rising from bonfires with diamond tongues.
The timeless prophecy spurts up,
tears a great O from all these throats as now
the comet shoots above our heads.
So greet a new Prometheus,
firebird soaring in the sky
where red plumes blossom, silver wheels
turn swiftly, falter and fade
while sounds are grey in a sulphur dark.

So lights fade over the water,
new planets slow their circling dance,
silent now beneath the powdery stars,
our eagles of paper and all the sudden
strangely beautiful birds
breaking phoenix-like from fire
and the moment's flight of our far desire.

Yet now we can wait and listen, for
'The Lord was not in the fire;
and after the fire a still small voice...'
a voice so hard to hear,
yet closer than we know.

THE STRANGER KINGS

That they should trespass on her winter thought,
ride unnoticed over the treeless plain
that filled the picture's corner, silently gain
the stable where the artist's work had brought
only a hint of perspective, yet taught
miracle and peace in a woman's pain –
the angels are silent, will never explain
the stranger kings, nor why their stay was short.

Nor can they tell how long the star burned;
astronomers have theorised but know
only half the story. Still and grey
came morning when the wondering strangers turned
silently towards the circling snow.
They took their lanterns, somehow found the way.

LATE EASTER

Better when Easter is late,
leaning on April away from winter;
else in our cold country
spring comes lentenly and slow.

Straggling early to church,
holding our hats uphill
against the wind
we still believe the story:
the stone rolled away
and the linen clothes folded inside.
But when rain thuds down on the porch
and yews cringe against the belfry
we need to think of spring,
that hidden prelude to its sudden green,
then the first leaf when the wind was still,
slow tree-glory breaking and branching,
gleaming on crowded fern and flower,
climbing tall to the sun.

So with April-Easter,
and the cherry in flower,
when blackbirds add
more magic to our psalms,
leaves are like gems and clouds
hang crystals to our wondering,
the vision glows from world to world,
the stone rolls back on resurrected spring,
we see the angel standing by the tomb.

A BAND IN THE PARK

These are for peace,
for sunshine and the circling chairs.
Scarlet is always their colour,
geranium-like in their painted stand.

His white gloves
lead them in jigs and conventional airs,
those quiet Sunday soldiers
with no sword in their tuneful hands.

NEW YEAR

People are suddenly tall and golden,
walking lightly in the winter street.
Now when the frozen roof-tops burn
sun is the warmth of a traveller's greeting –
however long
     long it is lost
love is the vision and must return.

Light is too bright when darkness is over,
spring is a lesson we all must learn,
wisdom the season that none can attack
on the white day of the new year turning –
however cold
     cold in our heart
joy is the echo and must look back.

Days burn low in a silver smoke,
people are older and fire-tossed,
but warmer their dream no eyes discern
for through the green of flowers frosting –
however long
     long it is lost
love is the vision and must return.

THE SMALLEST ORB

Reading this poetry at school
the cloudiness was firmly thumbed away
and past the boney diagrams in chalk
the dreaming cleared about the fleshless hills,
baring even that 'smallest orb…
But in his motion like an angel sings,
Still quiring to the young-eyed cherubins'*
to become the indefinite cross on the shallow ellipse.

Coldly worded the teacher's hand
lexiconed the music of the spheres,
that while we live, rooted so close to earth,
we cannot know, hearing but mortally;
instinctive then to waiting ears,
to ciphered wonder only read in death,
music awoke beyond the grammared heart,
briefly, with silence after swan-singing.

Then through the painful mazing years
this only held, was Ariadne to
the watching Theseus-mind, daring to reach
such monster-haunted core of life. The sudden
beacon burnt down smoky, when the thread
had broken in desire. Ariadne,
wounded in her love, saw music hang
its slow black sails across the empty sea.

Naxos released her to constell
the sky, crowned richer by a thoughtless hand
and unglossed oracle. No astronomy
can codify the spheres, transpose their song –
but all the whirling crystal world spins
white-hot in nerve and flesh. Behind our want,
beyond our rhetoric, briefly we hear
that singing from a rediscovered silence.

The Merchant of Venice, V, 1. 60-2.

AT SEASON'S TURN

Meeting now at season's turn
in a tall town where
crowd-faces flow to an empty shore,
passing thin gleam of elm
or beckon of chestnut
as April warms, then trespass in Xanadu,
without warning wander to
another world; boldly we reach those long green days
of ecstasy, snatching a fantasy of daffodils,
but watching no farther than
swan's wing shaken or
smudging of blossom against
the laurel's dark, now meet the ring of sheltering night
where only blackened ash-buds break;
and these, lighting an older world,
its core of stone, shine close
where blood-fraught jewels glow
through centuries of darkened fire.

We are more distant in the gleam
of spring than ever winter
dragged us into storm.
Walking through those April gardens,
taking hold of invisible hands,
absence meets the moment's voice.
The turning season holds its glass:
we are the crowd-face with empty eyes.

A LATE WORD FOR CHRISTMAS

A late word for Christmas
bringing some green warmth
to the secret talk of winter,
and you, my friends,
how cold would be winter without your voices,
darker than even that distant night
with its hard compelling star.
Your voices call from near and far
quick and fleeting as a mistletoe kiss,
drawing us now to the tranquil
and wondering thought of strange kings
in a strange country.

But soon each man is a different king,
each girl his queen in a blue dress,
welcoming golden gifts,
richer than any throne
or any watching moon;
evergreen as the holly
with its crinkled edge of love
that brings our greeting now with a late word,
a loving word for Christmas.

THE MOTHER

Who will see her on their journey,
waiting there beyond the bridge,
lonely out in the sun where
children wave to the roaring train?

Who will hear her when her words
go by like stations with half-seen names,
known to be picturesque
but not important, soon forgotten?

How far now her village garden,
the orchard with the golden pears.
Trains pass, and smoke
floats on the image of her face.

SLEEPING ON THE SOFA

A cat may look at a clock
and if in floating hours of dark
time was no rock
to climb on,
that black and brown and silent head
observed the chime
that led the night to day.

His shape the cairn
that crowns our solitude.
His stillness carves a friendly path
to landscapes in a wintry night.
All this in other distant lives
but where the stony steps lead back
a cat sill looks at a clock.

LEVIATHAN

In the great ocean of mysterious life
whales are the dream to swing our being's tide.
Huge and rare they move among the pride
of continents, the ice-floes and the trails of
sunset, shouldering thunder, breaking gales,
philosophers of storm. They school inside
our life, but with the anguished parricide
of monsters kill us when our courage fails.

Escaping shipwreck and the prize doubloon,
transformed leviathan abides for pity.
Defying any barb of man's harpoon
a travelling saint looked for his tranquil city:
Brendan, anchored in eternity,
close to his distant gods and a sea-wrack moon.

SOUVENIR DE LA MALMAISON

The name of the rose can never be lost,
and near the end the Emperor said:
'She was the only one I loved –
later, I had no time.'
The others, who seemed important,
loving perhaps, and lovelier,
did not really matter.
She, who was older,
spoke of love, and having learnt,
he found the strength to take a world.
Later, because the world was his,
she was the one he had to lose.
And later still, in the last island talk,
there were no battles that he had not won.

But was she closer to him still,
who grew the roses for an empty house?